With Best Wishes

Moira Andrew

Line Drawings by Andrea Heath
First published in 1992 by
BELAIR PUBLICATIONS LTD.
P. O. Box 12, Twickenham, England TW1 2QL

Series Editor Robyn Gordon
Series Designer Richard Souper
Photography by Kelvin Freeman
Typesetting by Belair
Printed and Bound in Ho[ng Kong by ... P]rint Ltd

INTRODUCTION

Many of our special occasion days are made more special by the giving and receiving of cards. Every child is familiar with cards to celebrate birthdays, Christmas and Mother's Day and understands how important it is to receive Get Well and Thank You cards. The ideas in this book extend the possibilities into other exciting occasions and suggest ways in which children can add individual touches to a basic design.

Most of the designs use easily available materials: thin card or art-weight papers, felt tip pens, glue and scissors, coloured tissue paper, foil, doilies, with scraps of wrapping paper, ribbon and lace, sequins, beads and cut-out magazine pictures. Some of the collage type cards use cereal packets as backing.

In the classroom the teacher may be able to offer a range of outline ideas which the children can finish and decorate in their own way. Parents are usually delighted to receive cards made and signed by their children — for individuality they far outshine the more sophisticated mass-produced products — and give them pride of place amongst the other cards on display.

At home, card-making can be relatively easy as it uses a range of simple materials and it provides a profitable way of channelling children's new-found skills in writing and drawing. Children's writing and artwork are enhanced when they are produced with the idea of audience in mind. Cards provide a vehicle for early handwriting skills and are seen by the children as a good reason for best handwriting.

Card-making provides an ideal opportunity for children to develop their design-technology skills. Pull-out, open-up and pop-up styles in particular require children to work out a strategy to make the card 'move'. Many of the cards can help teach older children the safe way to use a trimmer, sharp-pointed scissors or a craft knife with increasing independence.

Children can also be encouraged to explore different techniques — collage, pattern-making, blot-painting — as their card-making skills develop.

My thanks are due to the children of Malpas Park Primary School, Dinas Powys Infant School and Llansannor Church in Wales Primary School, for their help in making the cards which illustrate this book.

Moira Andrew

CONTENTS

SIMPLE FOLD CARDS

Simple folded cards can be made for all occasions and are perhaps the easiest to cope with in the classroom. They are very versatile and allow for many individual touches.

Use the front page for a standard greeting (Get Well, Congratulations, Bar Mitzvah, Happy Birthday, Good Luck), and the inside for the child's personal message. Felt-tip pens can be used to great effect.

● Get Well: First use wax crayons on white paper, filling random shapes with colour (in the style of 'taking a line for a walk'). Then outline letters for the greeting, cut out and glue to the outside of a simple fold of black card.

● Congratulations: Take a slanting shape, e.g. mountain, church spire or (as in the photograph) a ship's sail and outline the greeting in individual letters along the edge.

● Bar Mitzvah: Use silver marker pen on white card. Make a feature of the number 13 and add thirteen candles.

SIMPLE FOLD CARDS

● For a more sophisticated result, cut and paste illustrations first drawn on plain paper as in the clown card. Lisa found beads shaped like tears for the sad face on the cover and her finished card almost tells a story.

● The New Baby 'washing line' was suggested by small plastic pegs which can be bought in a stationery store. David looped string through holes strengthened by reinforcement rings, added green tissue 'grass' and 'nappies' cut from Dad's old white handkerchief to make a very personal New Baby card.

PULL-UP CARDS

Pull-up cards are a variation on the simple fold. For the front cover, choose a scene in which a figure can be hidden: an underwater scene with a diver or a mermaid for a Happy Holiday card; a spaceship with an astronaut for a Bon Voyage; or a chimney with a Father Christmas, as shown opposite.

Make a slit top and bottom and cut the figures from another piece of card. Just enough of the pull-through should be visible to make one want to see what it is! Make sure that there is a tab (or use the feet) to stop the figure being pulled right out.

● The Get Well card has a child in bed. Pull her up and her smiling face can be seen. The greeting is printed inside.

PULL-UP CARDS

● The Christmas card has Father Christmas wedged in a chimney. Again, the message is inside.

● Make a Welcome to a New Baby card in the same way with a baby hidden in a basket.

● Make a pretty Anniversary card or a Wedding Day card by hiding a bouquet of flowers inside a wrapping made from paper doilies.

● Hide ice-cream cones behind the picture of a deck chair; hide Punch and Judy behind a striped tent; hide fireworks made from scraps of coloured foil behind a picket fence for an unusual birthday or anniversary pull-up card.

ZIG-ZAG CARDS

Zig-zags are made by folding thin card into a concertina shape. (Use a tall zig-zag for a giraffe; a wide zig-zag for the elephant.)

● Elephant tells the sad tale of a forgotten birthday. The elephant shapes are cut from grey paper, pasted on and decorated with felt-tip pens and silver sequin tears.

ZIG-ZAG CARDS

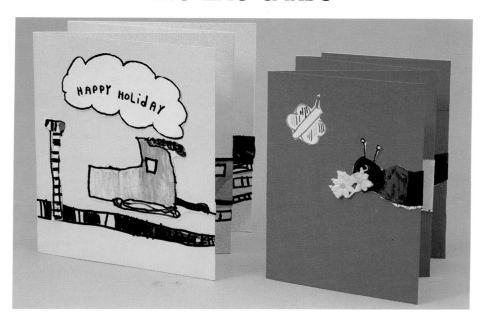

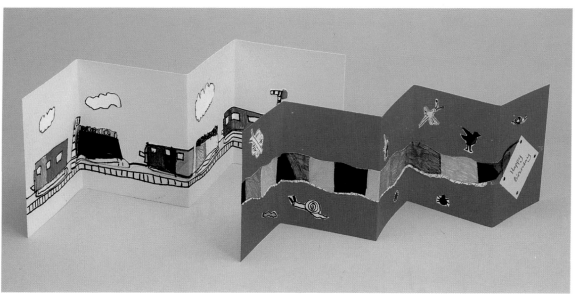

● The Bon Voyage train and caterpillar birthday card are first drawn and cut from plain paper, then pasted in place.

ZIG-ZAG CARDS

● The wedding bouquet uses flower shapes cut from a white doiley with yellow felt-tip pen centres, cut out and pasted in place. A red bow is added.

ZIG-ZAG CARDS

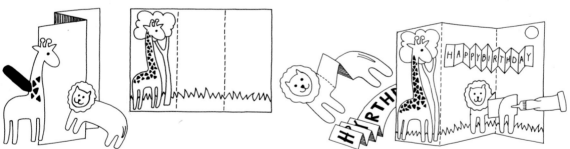

● Giraffe and lion shapes are first drawn to size on orange sugar paper, then cut and pasted as shown. The greeting is written across a concertina made from thin card.

● Zig-zag cards can make use of other long shapes e.g. snakes, a tug-of-war rope with a get-well wish on the end, trucks loaded with Christmas gifts, children joining hands holding out a Best Wishes message, or a set of triangular flags spelling out a greeting across the folds.

STAND-UP CARDS

Use a stand-up either as a greeting card or as part of a table display, e.g. for figures in a Nativity scene.

It is important to use an upright shape for the motif, e.g. tree, church, mountain. A standing figure is ideal — for Christmas use Mary or Joseph, a King or a shepherd, Father Christmas or a snowman (as illustrated).

STAND-UP CARDS

● To make the snowman, use two sheets of contrasting card cut into rectangles, one a little smaller than the other. Paint or draw the snowman figure on the smaller sheet, then glue to the background. Cut out and fold as shown.

● The card celebrating Mother's Day uses the same technique. A tree was drawn on white card and three different shades of green felt-tip pens were used to colour the tightly-packed leaves. The tree shape was then glued to a red backing sheet, cut out and folded to stand upright.

● The Christmas card is made from a simple triangular shape.

CORNER CARDS

Use a corner card to hold dried flowers, lollipops, finger puppets, flags, pencils — things which can be half-hidden in the folded-down corner.

● The number on the birthday card for a four-year-old is made from silver foil tape and the greeting is in silver pen to match. Lollies are held in place with adhesive tape.

CORNER CARDS

● Anniversary, Mother's Day or Birthday cards look most effective with dried flowers in the pocket as in the Thank You card.

● Hide silver heart shapes inside a red corner card for an unusual Valentine card.

● For small personal birthday gifts which have to go by post, make use of corner cards to hold a bookmark, a pretty handkerchief or a book of stamps.

● Another way of saying 'Thank you' is to tuck a little hand-written card in a contrasting colour into the corner pocket. Use newspaper or magazine letters pasted on the main card at random, like 'alphabet soup', to decorate the cover.

OPEN-UP CARDS

The butterfly is first designed in outline and the wings cut open. Then it is decorated using blot painting by dabbing blobs of colour on one wing and carefully blotting the other to get a symmetrical effect. When the wings are dry, use felt-tip pens to draw the body and print the greeting. Draw or paint a picture of summer flowers inside the card.

● Use the same idea to make dragon-fly or humming bird designs. Draw a pond scene inside the dragonfly card; bright jungle-type flowers inside the humming bird card. Use these cards for Thank You, Father's Day or anniversary messages.

OPEN-UP CARDS

The secret box uses the same technique as the butterfly card. Use two squares of card. Decorate the top square using felt-tip pens. Cut open the 'box lid' almost corner to corner. Glue the squares together round the edges and open the flaps to reveal the Happy Birthday message.

● Use the secret box idea to hide any greeting — Valentine, Thank You, Good Luck, Get Well etc.

17

HANG-UP CARDS

Use simple shapes to make hang-up cards. Cut out two matching shapes so that the loop is held between them.

● The heart-shaped Valentine cards are made to hang from a dressing table or mirror. The blue card uses hand-made paper and is edged with lace. The cream card is decorated with roses cut from a scrap of embroidery ribbon. Both are backed with card cut from cereal packets.

● The Good Luck cat is decorated with silver pen. His whiskers are made from dried flower stems.

● The Christmas baubles are made from cheese boxes and decorated with foil tape. They are simple enough for the youngest children to make.

● Make hang-up Easter eggs; silver foil flowers for Mother's Day; Christmas boxes from scraps of bright wrapping paper.

POP-UP CARDS

Although the pop-up uses one of the more difficult techniques, children have a great deal of fun making these cards.

The simple version shown above is made using a folded doiley with the gift taped inside.

● Use the pop-up feature to hold a spray of dried flowers to make a pretty card to celebrate Mother's Day, an anniversary or a birthday. It could even hold a lacy handkerchief or a tiny book of poems as a special present.

POP-UP CARDS

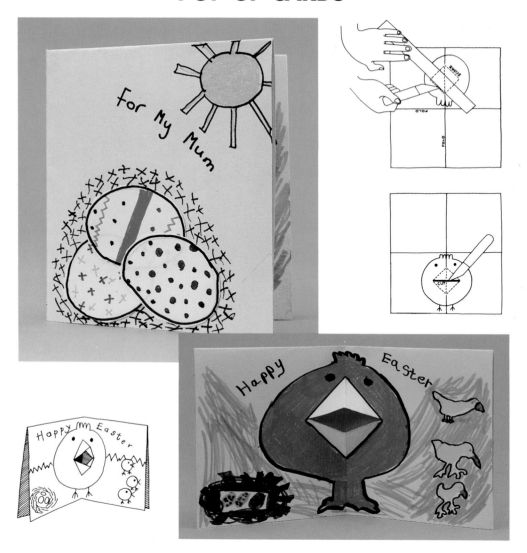

Use thin card folded in four, score and cut out the pop-up as shown. It can be made into the mouth of a fierce lion guarding the 'secret' of the card, a crocodile, a tiger or the beak of a bird.

● Give the Easter chicken a wide-open beak. Paste a scrap of red tissue behind the mouth for the best effect.

● Use the pop-up as a gateway to the garden for a New House card; as a stork's beak for a New Baby; as an opening box with red hearts hidden inside for a Valentine.

DOOR AND WINDOW CARDS

Doors and windows are used for 'inside/outside' cards which half-hide a scene. They are the ideal format for a New Home greeting.

Use a simple fold with an opening door or window on the front cover.

● The door card opens to a cosy indoor scene with a Happy Moving Day message.

● The gate opens to a garden bright with flowers and another New Home greeting.

● The window is more complicated with the opening cut away and backed with a clear Cellophane sheet. Then strips of black paper have been criss-crossed to give a trellis effect. Inside is a simple vase of flowers, first drawn on white paper, using felt-tip pens, then cut and pasted inside.

● Use this idea with a stable scene for a Christmas card; as a lid opening on a present for a Birthday card; as a porthole on a ship for a Bon Voyage card.

HOUSE CARDS

Take a rectangle of card and fold sides to middle so that it stands upright. Cut the top into a roof shape and decorate the front like a house. Cut round the windows to make them open.

● The stable scene opens to reveal cut-out shapes of Mary and Joseph and the baby Jesus. It is a style easy enough for young children to attempt.

● Make a car card in the same way. Have it open up to read 'Congratulations on Passing Your Driving Test'.

● Use the house card for a New Home message.

● Make a school or college opening card with 'Congratulations on Passing Your Exams'.

● Make a church in the same way. Open it up to show a picture of the bride and groom with a Wedding Day greeting.

FRAME CARDS

This style provides an environment for the scene shown on the card. It has something of a three dimensional effect and is ideal for a 'Welcome to Your New Home' card.

The frame card illustrated has been made to celebrate Divali, the Festival of Lights. The border has been filled with overlapping tissue paper flames pasted flat, and the inside shows all kinds of lights, drawn and coloured in felt-tip pens.

● For a New House card, fill the frame collage-style with leaves and flowers, either cut from magazine pictures or drawn on white paper and cut out. Draw the new house and add the greeting on the inside page.

● For a Bon Voyage card make a collage of holiday items around the frame and draw a ship or aeroplane on the inside.

● For a birthday card have birds, animals, flowers and leaves, as in a hedgerow, on the frame, with a countryside scene of hills and fields inside.

● For a new baby, fill the frame with bootees, rattles, bibs and toys with a baby in a basket shown inside along with the message.

SHAPE CARDS

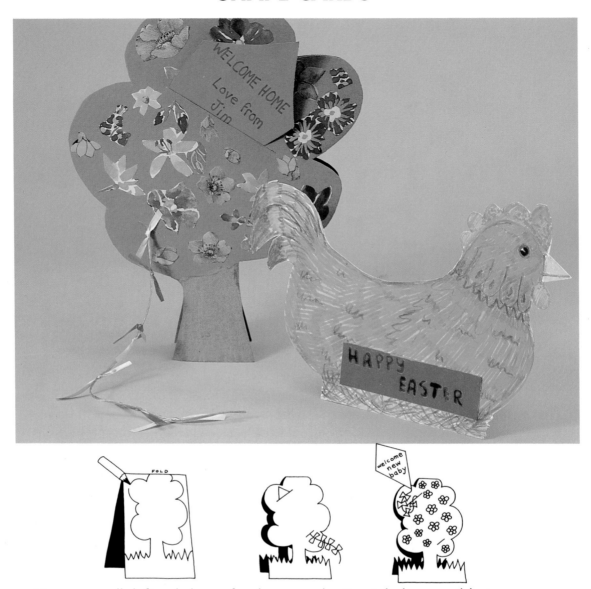

Use any well-defined shape for these cards. (It might be possible to use commercial templates for the outlines.) Try trains, railway engines, trees, houses etc.

Cut the cards double with the fold at the top, so that the cards will be free-standing.

● The Welcome Home tree uses wrapping paper cut-outs for blossom. The greeting is printed across a kite made from a separate piece of card and slotted through the tree shape. Pull up the kite to read the message. Tape a string to the back and decorate with knots of coloured ribbon.

SHAPE CARDS

● Use a number outline to make a birthday card. On the Five card above, the number was made using ribbon which had decorated a birthday cake, cut into strips and pasted into place (with a little adult help).

● Make a Bon Voyage card from a coach or train with children waving from the windows. The bus has cut-out windows, backed in black card. Each window shows a figure drawn in felt-tip pens on white paper, cut and pasted into place, collage fashion.

● The Thank You card uses alphabet templates to spell out the word, with the letters then built up one on top of the other, coloured with felt-tip pens, then cut around to make a shaped outline. The same idea could be used for Best Wishes, Good Luck, Congratulations.

● Use egg shapes or chickens for Easter greetings, fir trees or sleighs for Christmas, candle or lantern shapes for Divali.

● Make Welcome to Your New Home cards from house shapes.

FLAP CARDS

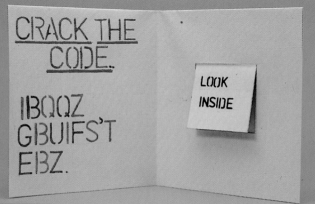

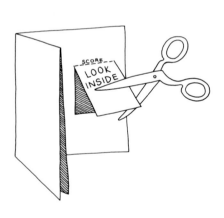

Flap cards hide some kind of secret — a message, a picture, a tiny gift.

To make a flap card use a rectangle of thin card folded into four, as shown. Note that the folded edge must be at the top. Put the greeting on the front, add your personal message inside the front cover and make an opening flap on the right-hand page. Hide a 'secret' beneath the flap.

● For an unusual Father's Day card, devise a secret code to keep your father guessing, as in the card above. The front cover suggests a SECRET MISSION, the following page is in code, and the solution is hidden under the flap.

FLAP CARDS

● The Wedding Day card has gold rings hidden in a secret box with the flap an opening lid.

● Make a Valentine card with red hearts to be found under the flap.

● Make a birthday or Thank You card for grandmother with the flap designed as a picture frame or locket with a tiny photograph of the sender hidden inside.

● Hide a posy of dried flowers beneath the flap as a surprise gift for an anniversary or Mother's Day card.

PULL-OUT CARDS

The pull-out card has a paper mechanism which alternately hides and displays a picture. Children enjoy working out ways to make it move.

As illustrated, the basis of this style of card is a rectangle folded into four with the folded edge at the top. A strip of card is fitted through slots, so that it can be pulled out to reveal a new picture.

● The birthday card has a greeting in gold pen on the cover. Look inside and there is a cloudy sky with lots of rain. Pull out the strip and magically it changes to a rainbow with a pot of gold. Use felt-tip pens and lots of gold sequins.

PULL-OUT CARDS

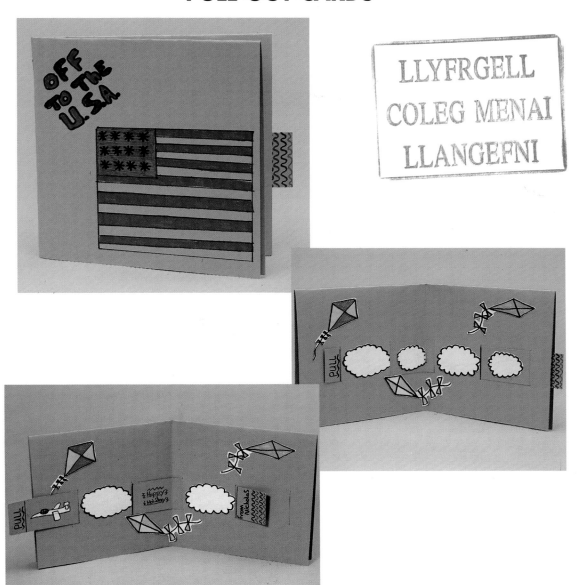

● The Bon Voyage card shows clouds and kites, all first drawn on white paper, coloured and cut out. Pull out the strip and the aeroplane flies across the sky, trailing its 'Happy Holiday' greeting.

● Use this technique to show Father Christmas riding in his sleigh across a dark starry sky.

● Draw or paint a seascape with bright yachts, mermaids or King Neptune hidden beneath the waves trailing a Bon Voyage message.

ENVELOPE CARDS

 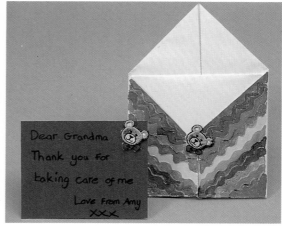

The envelope can be made origami style from any A4-size paper or thin card. It is ideal for holding a tiny Thank You card, a very personal birthday or anniversary note.

Make the envelope as illustrated on the opposite page and finish off with a motif pasted on the front to hold the whole thing together. (I am grateful to Paul Johnson for this design in *A Book of One's Own*, Hodder & Stoughton.)

● The Thank You card neatly fits into an envelope made from an A4 sheet patterned in felt-tip. It has just enough space to take Amy's thanks to grandmother for looking after her. The bear is a sewing motif bought with a number of other ends-of-line at the local market.

● The silver and red envelope is made from a scrap of leftover wrapping paper. The flowers are cut from a doiley coloured in gold and silver inks, then glued into a bouquet shape. The text reads 'Best Wishes'.

ENVELOPE CARDS

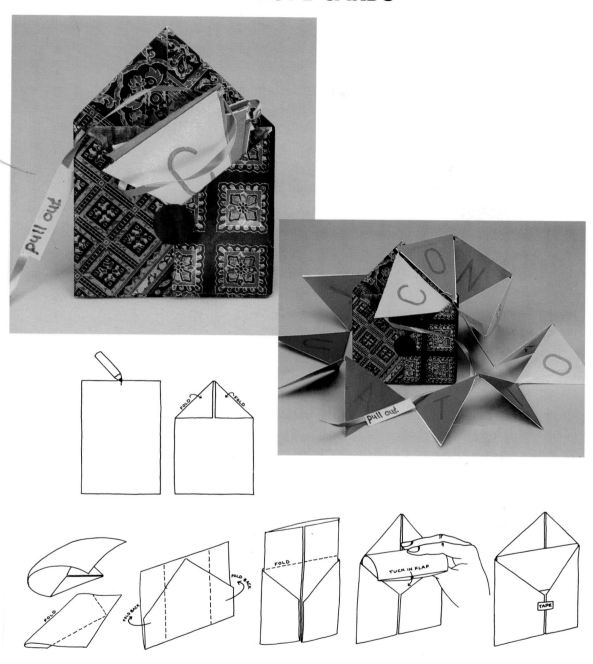

● Another use for the envelope is to conceal a banner which spells out a CONGRATULATIONS message. Each letter of the banner is stencilled on coloured gummed paper, cut into a diamond shape, then folded over a ribbon and taped to the inside of the envelope. Any greeting can be made up in this way. (Note that the last letter of the banner should be on the right-hand side of the ribbon so that it reads from the left.)

31

BOOK-IN-A-BAG

This is a very special Mother's Day card. Hannah wrote a poem about her mother, thinking of her 'through the senses'. She then made her poem into a tiny book and fitted it into a matching bag made from wrapping paper (see instructions on the previous page). The cover of the book is decorated with a pressed flower.

● This idea can be used for Wedding Day poems, Get Well poems or verses for Valentine's Day.

Hannah's poem:

```
My Mum

My Mum smells of music
My Mum tastes of sugar
My Mum looks like roses
My Mum sounds like the morning
My Mum feels like petals
My Mum's marvellous
brilliant
and the greatest
And I LOVE her.
```